WHAT'S MY PASSWORD?

Keep track of passwords, logins, websites & subscriptions.

COPYRIGHT © 2018

A

A

Name	
Web Address	
Login/Username	
Password	
Security Question(s)	
Date Last changed	
Notes	

Name	
Web Address	
Login/Username	
Password	
Security Question(s)	
Date Last changed	
Notes	

A

Name	
Web Address	
Login/Username	
Password	
Security Question(s)	
Date Last changed	
Notes	

Name	
Web Address	
Login/Username	
Password	
Security Question(s)	
Date Last changed	
Notes	

A

Name	
Web Address	
Login/Username	
Password	
Security Question(s)	
Date Last changed	
Notes	

Name	
Web Address	
Login/Username	
Password	
Security Question(s)	
Date Last changed	
Notes	

A

Name	
Web Address	
Login/Username	
Password	
Security Question(s)	
Date Last changed	
Notes	

Name	
Web Address	
Login/Username	
Password	
Security Question(s)	
Date Last changed	
Notes	

A

Name	
Web Address	
Login/Username	
Password	
Security Question(s)	
Date Last changed	
Notes	

Name	
Web Address	
Login/Username	
Password	
Security Question(s)	
Date Last changed	
Notes	

A

Name	
Web Address	
Login/Username	
Password	
Security Question(s)	
Date Last changed	
Notes	

Name	
Web Address	
Login/Username	
Password	
Security Question(s)	
Date Last changed	
Notes	

A

Name	
Web Address	
Login/Username	
Password	
Security Question(s)	
Date Last changed	
Notes	

Name	
Web Address	
Login/Username	
Password	
Security Question(s)	
Date Last changed	
Notes	

B

B

Name	
Web Address	
Login/Username	
Password	
Security Question(s)	
Date Last changed	
Notes	

Name	
Web Address	
Login/Username	
Password	
Security Question(s)	
Date Last changed	
Notes	

B

Name	
Web Address	
Login/Username	
Password	
Security Question(s)	
Date Last changed	
Notes	

Name	
Web Address	
Login/Username	
Password	
Security Question(s)	
Date Last changed	
Notes	

B

Name	
Web Address	
Login/Username	
Password	
Security Question(s)	
Date Last changed	
Notes	

Name	
Web Address	
Login/Username	
Password	
Security Question(s)	
Date Last changed	
Notes	

B

Name	
Web Address	
Login/Username	
Password	
Security Question(s)	
Date Last changed	
Notes	

Name	
Web Address	
Login/Username	
Password	
Security Question(s)	
Date Last changed	
Notes	

B

Name	
Web Address	
Login/Username	
Password	
Security Question(s)	
Date Last changed	
Notes	

Name	
Web Address	
Login/Username	
Password	
Security Question(s)	
Date Last changed	
Notes	

B

Name	
Web Address	
Login/Username	
Password	
Security Question(s)	
Date Last changed	
Notes	

Name	
Web Address	
Login/Username	
Password	
Security Question(s)	
Date Last changed	
Notes	

B

Name	
Web Address	
Login/Username	
Password	
Security Question(s)	
Date Last changed	
Notes	

Name	
Web Address	
Login/Username	
Password	
Security Question(s)	
Date Last changed	
Notes	

C

Name	
Web Address	
Login/Username	
Password	
Security Question(s)	
Date Last changed	
Notes	

Name	
Web Address	
Login/Username	
Password	
Security Question(s)	
Date Last changed	
Notes	

C

Name	
Web Address	
Login/Username	
Password	
Security Question(s)	
Date Last changed	
Notes	

Name	
Web Address	
Login/Username	
Password	
Security Question(s)	
Date Last changed	
Notes	

C

Name	
Web Address	
Login/Username	
Password	
Security Question(s)	
Date Last changed	
Notes	

Name	
Web Address	
Login/Username	
Password	
Security Question(s)	
Date Last changed	
Notes	

C

Name	
Web Address	
Login/Username	
Password	
Security Question(s)	
Date Last changed	
Notes	

Name	
Web Address	
Login/Username	
Password	
Security Question(s)	
Date Last changed	
Notes	

C

Name	
Web Address	
Login/Username	
Password	
Security Question(s)	
Date Last changed	
Notes	

Name	
Web Address	
Login/Username	
Password	
Security Question(s)	
Date Last changed	
Notes	

C

Name	
Web Address	
Login/Username	
Password	
Security Question(s)	
Date Last changed	
Notes	

Name	
Web Address	
Login/Username	
Password	
Security Question(s)	
Date Last changed	
Notes	

C

Name	
Web Address	
Login/Username	
Password	
Security Question(s)	
Date Last changed	
Notes	

Name	
Web Address	
Login/Username	
Password	
Security Question(s)	
Date Last changed	
Notes	

D

D

Name	
Web Address	
Login/Username	
Password	
Security Question(s)	
Date Last changed	
Notes	

Name	
Web Address	
Login/Username	
Password	
Security Question(s)	
Date Last changed	
Notes	

D

Name	
Web Address	
Login/Username	
Password	
Security Question(s)	
Date Last changed	
Notes	

Name	
Web Address	
Login/Username	
Password	
Security Question(s)	
Date Last changed	
Notes	

D

Name	
Web Address	
Login/Username	
Password	
Security Question(s)	
Date Last changed	
Notes	

Name	
Web Address	
Login/Username	
Password	
Security Question(s)	
Date Last changed	
Notes	

D

Name	
Web Address	
Login/Username	
Password	
Security Question(s)	
Date Last changed	
Notes	

Name	
Web Address	
Login/Username	
Password	
Security Question(s)	
Date Last changed	
Notes	

D

Name	
Web Address	
Login/Username	
Password	
Security Question(s)	
Date Last changed	
Notes	

Name	
Web Address	
Login/Username	
Password	
Security Question(s)	
Date Last changed	
Notes	

D

Name	
Web Address	
Login/Username	
Password	
Security Question(s)	
Date Last changed	
Notes	

Name	
Web Address	
Login/Username	
Password	
Security Question(s)	
Date Last changed	
Notes	

D

Name	
Web Address	
Login/Username	
Password	
Security Question(s)	
Date Last changed	
Notes	

Name	
Web Address	
Login/Username	
Password	
Security Question(s)	
Date Last changed	
Notes	

E

E

Name	
Web Address	
Login/Username	
Password	
Security Question(s)	
Date Last changed	
Notes	

Name	
Web Address	
Login/Username	
Password	
Security Question(s)	
Date Last changed	
Notes	

E

Name	
Web Address	
Login/Username	
Password	
Security Question(s)	
Date Last changed	
Notes	

Name	
Web Address	
Login/Username	
Password	
Security Question(s)	
Date Last changed	
Notes	

E

Name	
Web Address	
Login/Username	
Password	
Security Question(s)	
Date Last changed	
Notes	

Name	
Web Address	
Login/Username	
Password	
Security Question(s)	
Date Last changed	
Notes	

E

Name	
Web Address	
Login/Username	
Password	
Security Question(s)	
Date Last changed	
Notes	

Name	
Web Address	
Login/Username	
Password	
Security Question(s)	
Date Last changed	
Notes	

E

Name	
Web Address	
Login/Username	
Password	
Security Question(s)	
Date Last changed	
Notes	

Name	
Web Address	
Login/Username	
Password	
Security Question(s)	
Date Last changed	
Notes	

E

Name	
Web Address	
Login/Username	
Password	
Security Question(s)	
Date Last changed	
Notes	

Name	
Web Address	
Login/Username	
Password	
Security Question(s)	
Date Last changed	
Notes	

E

Name	
Web Address	
Login/Username	
Password	
Security Question(s)	
Date Last changed	
Notes	

Name	
Web Address	
Login/Username	
Password	
Security Question(s)	
Date Last changed	
Notes	

F

Name	
Web Address	
Login/Username	
Password	
Security Question(s)	
Date Last changed	
Notes	

Name	
Web Address	
Login/Username	
Password	
Security Question(s)	
Date Last changed	
Notes	

F

Name	
Web Address	
Login/Username	
Password	
Security Question(s)	
Date Last changed	
Notes	

Name	
Web Address	
Login/Username	
Password	
Security Question(s)	
Date Last changed	
Notes	

F

Name	
Web Address	
Login/Username	
Password	
Security Question(s)	
Date Last changed	
Notes	

Name	
Web Address	
Login/Username	
Password	
Security Question(s)	
Date Last changed	
Notes	

F

Name	
Web Address	
Login/Username	
Password	
Security Question(s)	
Date Last changed	
Notes	

Name	
Web Address	
Login/Username	
Password	
Security Question(s)	
Date Last changed	
Notes	

F

Name	
Web Address	
Login/Username	
Password	
Security Question(s)	
Date Last changed	
Notes	

Name	
Web Address	
Login/Username	
Password	
Security Question(s)	
Date Last changed	
Notes	

F

Name	
Web Address	
Login/Username	
Password	
Security Question(s)	
Date Last changed	
Notes	

Name	
Web Address	
Login/Username	
Password	
Security Question(s)	
Date Last changed	
Notes	

F

Name	
Web Address	
Login/Username	
Password	
Security Question(s)	
Date Last changed	
Notes	

Name	
Web Address	
Login/Username	
Password	
Security Question(s)	
Date Last changed	
Notes	

G

G

Name	
Web Address	
Login/Username	
Password	
Security Question(s)	
Date Last changed	
Notes	

Name	
Web Address	
Login/Username	
Password	
Security Question(s)	
Date Last changed	
Notes	

G

Name	
Web Address	
Login/Username	
Password	
Security Question(s)	
Date Last changed	
Notes	

Name	
Web Address	
Login/Username	
Password	
Security Question(s)	
Date Last changed	
Notes	

G

Name	
Web Address	
Login/Username	
Password	
Security Question(s)	
Date Last changed	
Notes	

Name	
Web Address	
Login/Username	
Password	
Security Question(s)	
Date Last changed	
Notes	

G

Name	
Web Address	
Login/Username	
Password	
Security Question(s)	
Date Last changed	
Notes	

Name	
Web Address	
Login/Username	
Password	
Security Question(s)	
Date Last changed	
Notes	

G

Name	
Web Address	
Login/Username	
Password	
Security Question(s)	
Date Last changed	
Notes	

Name	
Web Address	
Login/Username	
Password	
Security Question(s)	
Date Last changed	
Notes	

G

Name	
Web Address	
Login/Username	
Password	
Security Question(s)	
Date Last changed	
Notes	

Name	
Web Address	
Login/Username	
Password	
Security Question(s)	
Date Last changed	
Notes	

G

Name	
Web Address	
Login/Username	
Password	
Security Question(s)	
Date Last changed	
Notes	

Name	
Web Address	
Login/Username	
Password	
Security Question(s)	
Date Last changed	
Notes	

H

H

Name	
Web Address	
Login/Username	
Password	
Security Question(s)	
Date Last changed	
Notes	

Name	
Web Address	
Login/Username	
Password	
Security Question(s)	
Date Last changed	
Notes	

H

Name	
Web Address	
Login/Username	
Password	
Security Question(s)	
Date Last changed	
Notes	

Name	
Web Address	
Login/Username	
Password	
Security Question(s)	
Date Last changed	
Notes	

H

Name	
Web Address	
Login/Username	
Password	
Security Question(s)	
Date Last changed	
Notes	

Name	
Web Address	
Login/Username	
Password	
Security Question(s)	
Date Last changed	
Notes	

H

Name	
Web Address	
Login/Username	
Password	
Security Question(s)	
Date Last changed	
Notes	

Name	
Web Address	
Login/Username	
Password	
Security Question(s)	
Date Last changed	
Notes	

H

Name	
Web Address	
Login/Username	
Password	
Security Question(s)	
Date Last changed	
Notes	

Name	
Web Address	
Login/Username	
Password	
Security Question(s)	
Date Last changed	
Notes	

H

Name	
Web Address	
Login/Username	
Password	
Security Question(s)	
Date Last changed	
Notes	

Name	
Web Address	
Login/Username	
Password	
Security Question(s)	
Date Last changed	
Notes	

H

Name	
Web Address	
Login/Username	
Password	
Security Question(s)	
Date Last changed	
Notes	

Name	
Web Address	
Login/Username	
Password	
Security Question(s)	
Date Last changed	
Notes	

I

Name	
Web Address	
Login/Username	
Password	
Security Question(s)	
Date Last changed	
Notes	

Name	
Web Address	
Login/Username	
Password	
Security Question(s)	
Date Last changed	
Notes	

Name	
Web Address	
Login/Username	
Password	
Security Question(s)	
Date Last changed	
Notes	

Name	
Web Address	
Login/Username	
Password	
Security Question(s)	
Date Last changed	
Notes	

Name	
Web Address	
Login/Username	
Password	
Security Question(s)	
Date Last changed	
Notes	

Name	
Web Address	
Login/Username	
Password	
Security Question(s)	
Date Last changed	
Notes	

Name	
Web Address	
Login/Username	
Password	
Security Question(s)	
Date Last changed	
Notes	

Name	
Web Address	
Login/Username	
Password	
Security Question(s)	
Date Last changed	
Notes	

Name	
Web Address	
Login/Username	
Password	
Security Question(s)	
Date Last changed	
Notes	

Name	
Web Address	
Login/Username	
Password	
Security Question(s)	
Date Last changed	
Notes	

Name	
Web Address	
Login/Username	
Password	
Security Question(s)	
Date Last changed	
Notes	

Name	
Web Address	
Login/Username	
Password	
Security Question(s)	
Date Last changed	
Notes	

Name	
Web Address	
Login/Username	
Password	
Security Question(s)	
Date Last changed	
Notes	

Name	
Web Address	
Login/Username	
Password	
Security Question(s)	
Date Last changed	
Notes	

J

Name	
Web Address	
Login/Username	
Password	
Security Question(s)	
Date Last changed	
Notes	

Name	
Web Address	
Login/Username	
Password	
Security Question(s)	
Date Last changed	
Notes	

Name	
Web Address	
Login/Username	
Password	
Security Question(s)	
Date Last changed	
Notes	

Name	
Web Address	
Login/Username	
Password	
Security Question(s)	
Date Last changed	
Notes	

Name	
Web Address	
Login/Username	
Password	
Security Question(s)	
Date Last changed	
Notes	

Name	
Web Address	
Login/Username	
Password	
Security Question(s)	
Date Last changed	
Notes	

Name	
Web Address	
Login/Username	
Password	
Security Question(s)	
Date Last changed	
Notes	

Name	
Web Address	
Login/Username	
Password	
Security Question(s)	
Date Last changed	
Notes	

Name	
Web Address	
Login/Username	
Password	
Security Question(s)	
Date Last changed	
Notes	

Name	
Web Address	
Login/Username	
Password	
Security Question(s)	
Date Last changed	
Notes	

Name	
Web Address	
Login/Username	
Password	
Security Question(s)	
Date Last changed	
Notes	

Name	
Web Address	
Login/Username	
Password	
Security Question(s)	
Date Last changed	
Notes	

Name	
Web Address	
Login/Username	
Password	
Security Question(s)	
Date Last changed	
Notes	

Name	
Web Address	
Login/Username	
Password	
Security Question(s)	
Date Last changed	
Notes	

K

K

Name	
Web Address	
Login/Username	
Password	
Security Question(s)	
Date Last changed	
Notes	

Name	
Web Address	
Login/Username	
Password	
Security Question(s)	
Date Last changed	
Notes	

K

Name	
Web Address	
Login/Username	
Password	
Security Question(s)	
Date Last changed	
Notes	

Name	
Web Address	
Login/Username	
Password	
Security Question(s)	
Date Last changed	
Notes	

K

Name	
Web Address	
Login/Username	
Password	
Security Question(s)	
Date Last changed	
Notes	

Name	
Web Address	
Login/Username	
Password	
Security Question(s)	
Date Last changed	
Notes	

K

Name	
Web Address	
Login/Username	
Password	
Security Question(s)	
Date Last changed	
Notes	

Name	
Web Address	
Login/Username	
Password	
Security Question(s)	
Date Last changed	
Notes	

K

Name	
Web Address	
Login/Username	
Password	
Security Question(s)	
Date Last changed	
Notes	

Name	
Web Address	
Login/Username	
Password	
Security Question(s)	
Date Last changed	
Notes	

K

Name	
Web Address	
Login/Username	
Password	
Security Question(s)	
Date Last changed	
Notes	

Name	
Web Address	
Login/Username	
Password	
Security Question(s)	
Date Last changed	
Notes	

K

Name	
Web Address	
Login/Username	
Password	
Security Question(s)	
Date Last changed	
Notes	

Name	
Web Address	
Login/Username	
Password	
Security Question(s)	
Date Last changed	
Notes	

L

L

Name	
Web Address	
Login/Username	
Password	
Security Question(s)	
Date Last changed	
Notes	

Name	
Web Address	
Login/Username	
Password	
Security Question(s)	
Date Last changed	
Notes	

L

Name	
Web Address	
Login/Username	
Password	
Security Question(s)	
Date Last changed	
Notes	

Name	
Web Address	
Login/Username	
Password	
Security Question(s)	
Date Last changed	
Notes	

L

Name	
Web Address	
Login/Username	
Password	
Security Question(s)	
Date Last changed	
Notes	

Name	
Web Address	
Login/Username	
Password	
Security Question(s)	
Date Last changed	
Notes	

L

Name	
Web Address	
Login/Username	
Password	
Security Question(s)	
Date Last changed	
Notes	

Name	
Web Address	
Login/Username	
Password	
Security Question(s)	
Date Last changed	
Notes	

L

Name	
Web Address	
Login/Username	
Password	
Security Question(s)	
Date Last changed	
Notes	

Name	
Web Address	
Login/Username	
Password	
Security Question(s)	
Date Last changed	
Notes	

L

Name	
Web Address	
Login/Username	
Password	
Security Question(s)	
Date Last changed	
Notes	

Name	
Web Address	
Login/Username	
Password	
Security Question(s)	
Date Last changed	
Notes	

L

Name	
Web Address	
Login/Username	
Password	
Security Question(s)	
Date Last changed	
Notes	

Name	
Web Address	
Login/Username	
Password	
Security Question(s)	
Date Last changed	
Notes	

M

M

Name	
Web Address	
Login/Username	
Password	
Security Question(s)	
Date Last changed	
Notes	

Name	
Web Address	
Login/Username	
Password	
Security Question(s)	
Date Last changed	
Notes	

M

Name	
Web Address	
Login/Username	
Password	
Security Question(s)	
Date Last changed	
Notes	

Name	
Web Address	
Login/Username	
Password	
Security Question(s)	
Date Last changed	
Notes	

M

Name	
Web Address	
Login/Username	
Password	
Security Question(s)	
Date Last changed	
Notes	

Name	
Web Address	
Login/Username	
Password	
Security Question(s)	
Date Last changed	
Notes	

M

Name	
Web Address	
Login/Username	
Password	
Security Question(s)	
Date Last changed	
Notes	

Name	
Web Address	
Login/Username	
Password	
Security Question(s)	
Date Last changed	
Notes	

M

Name	
Web Address	
Login/Username	
Password	
Security Question(s)	
Date Last changed	
Notes	

Name	
Web Address	
Login/Username	
Password	
Security Question(s)	
Date Last changed	
Notes	

M

Name	
Web Address	
Login/Username	
Password	
Security Question(s)	
Date Last changed	
Notes	

Name	
Web Address	
Login/Username	
Password	
Security Question(s)	
Date Last changed	
Notes	

M

Name	
Web Address	
Login/Username	
Password	
Security Question(s)	
Date Last changed	
Notes	

Name	
Web Address	
Login/Username	
Password	
Security Question(s)	
Date Last changed	
Notes	

N

N

Name	
Web Address	
Login/Username	
Password	
Security Question(s)	
Date Last changed	
Notes	

Name	
Web Address	
Login/Username	
Password	
Security Question(s)	
Date Last changed	
Notes	

N

Name	
Web Address	
Login/Username	
Password	
Security Question(s)	
Date Last changed	
Notes	

Name	
Web Address	
Login/Username	
Password	
Security Question(s)	
Date Last changed	
Notes	

N

Name	
Web Address	
Login/Username	
Password	
Security Question(s)	
Date Last changed	
Notes	

Name	
Web Address	
Login/Username	
Password	
Security Question(s)	
Date Last changed	
Notes	

N

Name	
Web Address	
Login/Username	
Password	
Security Question(s)	
Date Last changed	
Notes	

Name	
Web Address	
Login/Username	
Password	
Security Question(s)	
Date Last changed	
Notes	

N

Name	
Web Address	
Login/Username	
Password	
Security Question(s)	
Date Last changed	
Notes	

Name	
Web Address	
Login/Username	
Password	
Security Question(s)	
Date Last changed	
Notes	

N

Name	
Web Address	
Login/Username	
Password	
Security Question(s)	
Date Last changed	
Notes	

Name	
Web Address	
Login/Username	
Password	
Security Question(s)	
Date Last changed	
Notes	

N

Name	
Web Address	
Login/Username	
Password	
Security Question(s)	
Date Last changed	
Notes	

Name	
Web Address	
Login/Username	
Password	
Security Question(s)	
Date Last changed	
Notes	

O

Name	
Web Address	
Login/Username	
Password	
Security Question(s)	
Date Last changed	
Notes	

Name	
Web Address	
Login/Username	
Password	
Security Question(s)	
Date Last changed	
Notes	

O

Name	
Web Address	
Login/Username	
Password	
Security Question(s)	
Date Last changed	
Notes	

Name	
Web Address	
Login/Username	
Password	
Security Question(s)	
Date Last changed	
Notes	

O

Name	
Web Address	
Login/Username	
Password	
Security Question(s)	
Date Last changed	
Notes	

Name	
Web Address	
Login/Username	
Password	
Security Question(s)	
Date Last changed	
Notes	

O

Name	
Web Address	
Login/Username	
Password	
Security Question(s)	
Date Last changed	
Notes	

Name	
Web Address	
Login/Username	
Password	
Security Question(s)	
Date Last changed	
Notes	

O

Name	
Web Address	
Login/Username	
Password	
Security Question(s)	
Date Last changed	
Notes	

Name	
Web Address	
Login/Username	
Password	
Security Question(s)	
Date Last changed	
Notes	

O

Name	
Web Address	
Login/Username	
Password	
Security Question(s)	
Date Last changed	
Notes	

Name	
Web Address	
Login/Username	
Password	
Security Question(s)	
Date Last changed	
Notes	

O

Name	
Web Address	
Login/Username	
Password	
Security Question(s)	
Date Last changed	
Notes	

Name	
Web Address	
Login/Username	
Password	
Security Question(s)	
Date Last changed	
Notes	

P-Q

Q

P-Q

Name	
Web Address	
Login/Username	
Password	
Security Question(s)	
Date Last changed	
Notes	

Name	
Web Address	
Login/Username	
Password	
Security Question(s)	
Date Last changed	
Notes	

P-Q

Name	
Web Address	
Login/Username	
Password	
Security Question(s)	
Date Last changed	
Notes	

Name	
Web Address	
Login/Username	
Password	
Security Question(s)	
Date Last changed	
Notes	

P-Q

Name	
Web Address	
Login/Username	
Password	
Security Question(s)	
Date Last changed	
Notes	

Name	
Web Address	
Login/Username	
Password	
Security Question(s)	
Date Last changed	
Notes	

P-Q

Name	
Web Address	
Login/Username	
Password	
Security Question(s)	
Date Last changed	
Notes	

Name	
Web Address	
Login/Username	
Password	
Security Question(s)	
Date Last changed	
Notes	

P-Q

Name	
Web Address	
Login/Username	
Password	
Security Question(s)	
Date Last changed	
Notes	

Name	
Web Address	
Login/Username	
Password	
Security Question(s)	
Date Last changed	
Notes	

P-Q

Name	
Web Address	
Login/Username	
Password	
Security Question(s)	
Date Last changed	
Notes	

Name	
Web Address	
Login/Username	
Password	
Security Question(s)	
Date Last changed	
Notes	

P-Q

Name	
Web Address	
Login/Username	
Password	
Security Question(s)	
Date Last changed	
Notes	

Name	
Web Address	
Login/Username	
Password	
Security Question(s)	
Date Last changed	
Notes	

R

R

Name	
Web Address	
Login/Username	
Password	
Security Question(s)	
Date Last changed	
Notes	

Name	
Web Address	
Login/Username	
Password	
Security Question(s)	
Date Last changed	
Notes	

R

Name	
Web Address	
Login/Username	
Password	
Security Question(s)	
Date Last changed	
Notes	

Name	
Web Address	
Login/Username	
Password	
Security Question(s)	
Date Last changed	
Notes	

R

Name	
Web Address	
Login/Username	
Password	
Security Question(s)	
Date Last changed	
Notes	

Name	
Web Address	
Login/Username	
Password	
Security Question(s)	
Date Last changed	
Notes	

R

Name	
Web Address	
Login/Username	
Password	
Security Question(s)	
Date Last changed	
Notes	

Name	
Web Address	
Login/Username	
Password	
Security Question(s)	
Date Last changed	
Notes	

R

Name	
Web Address	
Login/Username	
Password	
Security Question(s)	
Date Last changed	
Notes	

Name	
Web Address	
Login/Username	
Password	
Security Question(s)	
Date Last changed	
Notes	

R

Name	
Web Address	
Login/Username	
Password	
Security Question(s)	
Date Last changed	
Notes	

Name	
Web Address	
Login/Username	
Password	
Security Question(s)	
Date Last changed	
Notes	

R

Name	
Web Address	
Login/Username	
Password	
Security Question(s)	
Date Last changed	
Notes	

Name	
Web Address	
Login/Username	
Password	
Security Question(s)	
Date Last changed	
Notes	

S

S

Name	
Web Address	
Login/Username	
Password	
Security Question(s)	
Date Last changed	
Notes	

Name	
Web Address	
Login/Username	
Password	
Security Question(s)	
Date Last changed	
Notes	

S

Name	
Web Address	
Login/Username	
Password	
Security Question(s)	
Date Last changed	
Notes	

Name	
Web Address	
Login/Username	
Password	
Security Question(s)	
Date Last changed	
Notes	

S

Name	
Web Address	
Login/Username	
Password	
Security Question(s)	
Date Last changed	
Notes	

Name	
Web Address	
Login/Username	
Password	
Security Question(s)	
Date Last changed	
Notes	

S

Name	
Web Address	
Login/Username	
Password	
Security Question(s)	
Date Last changed	
Notes	

Name	
Web Address	
Login/Username	
Password	
Security Question(s)	
Date Last changed	
Notes	

S

Name	
Web Address	
Login/Username	
Password	
Security Question(s)	
Date Last changed	
Notes	

Name	
Web Address	
Login/Username	
Password	
Security Question(s)	
Date Last changed	
Notes	

S

Name	
Web Address	
Login/Username	
Password	
Security Question(s)	
Date Last changed	
Notes	

Name	
Web Address	
Login/Username	
Password	
Security Question(s)	
Date Last changed	
Notes	

S

Name	
Web Address	
Login/Username	
Password	
Security Question(s)	
Date Last changed	
Notes	

Name	
Web Address	
Login/Username	
Password	
Security Question(s)	
Date Last changed	
Notes	

T

T

Name	
Web Address	
Login/Username	
Password	
Security Question(s)	
Date Last changed	
Notes	

Name	
Web Address	
Login/Username	
Password	
Security Question(s)	
Date Last changed	
Notes	

T

Name	
Web Address	
Login/Username	
Password	
Security Question(s)	
Date Last changed	
Notes	

Name	
Web Address	
Login/Username	
Password	
Security Question(s)	
Date Last changed	
Notes	

T

Name	
Web Address	
Login/Username	
Password	
Security Question(s)	
Date Last changed	
Notes	

Name	
Web Address	
Login/Username	
Password	
Security Question(s)	
Date Last changed	
Notes	

T

Name	
Web Address	
Login/Username	
Password	
Security Question(s)	
Date Last changed	
Notes	

Name	
Web Address	
Login/Username	
Password	
Security Question(s)	
Date Last changed	
Notes	

T

Name	
Web Address	
Login/Username	
Password	
Security Question(s)	
Date Last changed	
Notes	

Name	
Web Address	
Login/Username	
Password	
Security Question(s)	
Date Last changed	
Notes	

T

Name	
Web Address	
Login/Username	
Password	
Security Question(s)	
Date Last changed	
Notes	

Name	
Web Address	
Login/Username	
Password	
Security Question(s)	
Date Last changed	
Notes	

T

Name	
Web Address	
Login/Username	
Password	
Security Question(s)	
Date Last changed	
Notes	

Name	
Web Address	
Login/Username	
Password	
Security Question(s)	
Date Last changed	
Notes	

U-V

U-V

Name	
Web Address	
Login/Username	
Password	
Security Question(s)	
Date Last changed	
Notes	

Name	
Web Address	
Login/Username	
Password	
Security Question(s)	
Date Last changed	
Notes	

U-V

Name	
Web Address	
Login/Username	
Password	
Security Question(s)	
Date Last changed	
Notes	

Name	
Web Address	
Login/Username	
Password	
Security Question(s)	
Date Last changed	
Notes	

U-V

Name	
Web Address	
Login/Username	
Password	
Security Question(s)	
Date Last changed	
Notes	

Name	
Web Address	
Login/Username	
Password	
Security Question(s)	
Date Last changed	
Notes	

U-V

Name	
Web Address	
Login/Username	
Password	
Security Question(s)	
Date Last changed	
Notes	

Name	
Web Address	
Login/Username	
Password	
Security Question(s)	
Date Last changed	
Notes	

U-V

Name	
Web Address	
Login/Username	
Password	
Security Question(s)	
Date Last changed	
Notes	

Name	
Web Address	
Login/Username	
Password	
Security Question(s)	
Date Last changed	
Notes	

U-V

Name	
Web Address	
Login/Username	
Password	
Security Question(s)	
Date Last changed	
Notes	

Name	
Web Address	
Login/Username	
Password	
Security Question(s)	
Date Last changed	
Notes	

U-V

Name	
Web Address	
Login/Username	
Password	
Security Question(s)	
Date Last changed	
Notes	

Name	
Web Address	
Login/Username	
Password	
Security Question(s)	
Date Last changed	
Notes	

W

Name	
Web Address	
Login/Username	
Password	
Security Question(s)	
Date Last changed	
Notes	

Name	
Web Address	
Login/Username	
Password	
Security Question(s)	
Date Last changed	
Notes	

Name	
Web Address	
Login/Username	
Password	
Security Question(s)	
Date Last changed	
Notes	

Name	
Web Address	
Login/Username	
Password	
Security Question(s)	
Date Last changed	
Notes	

Name	
Web Address	
Login/Username	
Password	
Security Question(s)	
Date Last changed	
Notes	

Name	
Web Address	
Login/Username	
Password	
Security Question(s)	
Date Last changed	
Notes	

Name	
Web Address	
Login/Username	
Password	
Security Question(s)	
Date Last changed	
Notes	

Name	
Web Address	
Login/Username	
Password	
Security Question(s)	
Date Last changed	
Notes	

Name	
Web Address	
Login/Username	
Password	
Security Question(s)	
Date Last changed	
Notes	

Name	
Web Address	
Login/Username	
Password	
Security Question(s)	
Date Last changed	
Notes	

W

Name	
Web Address	
Login/Username	
Password	
Security Question(s)	
Date Last changed	
Notes	

Name	
Web Address	
Login/Username	
Password	
Security Question(s)	
Date Last changed	
Notes	

Name	
Web Address	
Login/Username	
Password	
Security Question(s)	
Date Last changed	
Notes	

Name	
Web Address	
Login/Username	
Password	
Security Question(s)	
Date Last changed	
Notes	

# X-Y

X-Y

Name	
Web Address	
Login/Username	
Password	
Security Question(s)	
Date Last changed	
Notes	

Name	
Web Address	
Login/Username	
Password	
Security Question(s)	
Date Last changed	
Notes	

X-Y

Name	
Web Address	
Login/Username	
Password	
Security Question(s)	
Date Last changed	
Notes	

Name	
Web Address	
Login/Username	
Password	
Security Question(s)	
Date Last changed	
Notes	

X-Y

Name	
Web Address	
Login/Username	
Password	
Security Question(s)	
Date Last changed	
Notes	

Name	
Web Address	
Login/Username	
Password	
Security Question(s)	
Date Last changed	
Notes	

X-Y

Name	
Web Address	
Login/Username	
Password	
Security Question(s)	
Date Last changed	
Notes	

Name	
Web Address	
Login/Username	
Password	
Security Question(s)	
Date Last changed	
Notes	

X-Y

Name	
Web Address	
Login/Username	
Password	
Security Question(s)	
Date Last changed	
Notes	

Name	
Web Address	
Login/Username	
Password	
Security Question(s)	
Date Last changed	
Notes	

X-Y

Name	
Web Address	
Login/Username	
Password	
Security Question(s)	
Date Last changed	
Notes	

Name	
Web Address	
Login/Username	
Password	
Security Question(s)	
Date Last changed	
Notes	

X-Y

Name	
Web Address	
Login/Username	
Password	
Security Question(s)	
Date Last changed	
Notes	

Name	
Web Address	
Login/Username	
Password	
Security Question(s)	
Date Last changed	
Notes	

Z

Z

Name	
Web Address	
Login/Username	
Password	
Security Question(s)	
Date Last changed	
Notes	

Name	
Web Address	
Login/Username	
Password	
Security Question(s)	
Date Last changed	
Notes	

Z

Name	
Web Address	
Login/Username	
Password	
Security Question(s)	
Date Last changed	
Notes	

Name	
Web Address	
Login/Username	
Password	
Security Question(s)	
Date Last changed	
Notes	

Z

Name	
Web Address	
Login/Username	
Password	
Security Question(s)	
Date Last changed	
Notes	

Name	
Web Address	
Login/Username	
Password	
Security Question(s)	
Date Last changed	
Notes	

Z

Name	
Web Address	
Login/Username	
Password	
Security Question(s)	
Date Last changed	
Notes	

Name	
Web Address	
Login/Username	
Password	
Security Question(s)	
Date Last changed	
Notes	

Z

Name	
Web Address	
Login/Username	
Password	
Security Question(s)	
Date Last changed	
Notes	

Name	
Web Address	
Login/Username	
Password	
Security Question(s)	
Date Last changed	
Notes	

Z

Name	
Web Address	
Login/Username	
Password	
Security Question(s)	
Date Last changed	
Notes	

Name	
Web Address	
Login/Username	
Password	
Security Question(s)	
Date Last changed	
Notes	

Z

Name	
Web Address	
Login/Username	
Password	
Security Question(s)	
Date Last changed	
Notes	

Name	
Web Address	
Login/Username	
Password	
Security Question(s)	
Date Last changed	
Notes	

NOTES

Record the login and password of your home network, mobile phones, tablets and computers.

Serial and license numbers of all your programs and apps.

Subscriptions.

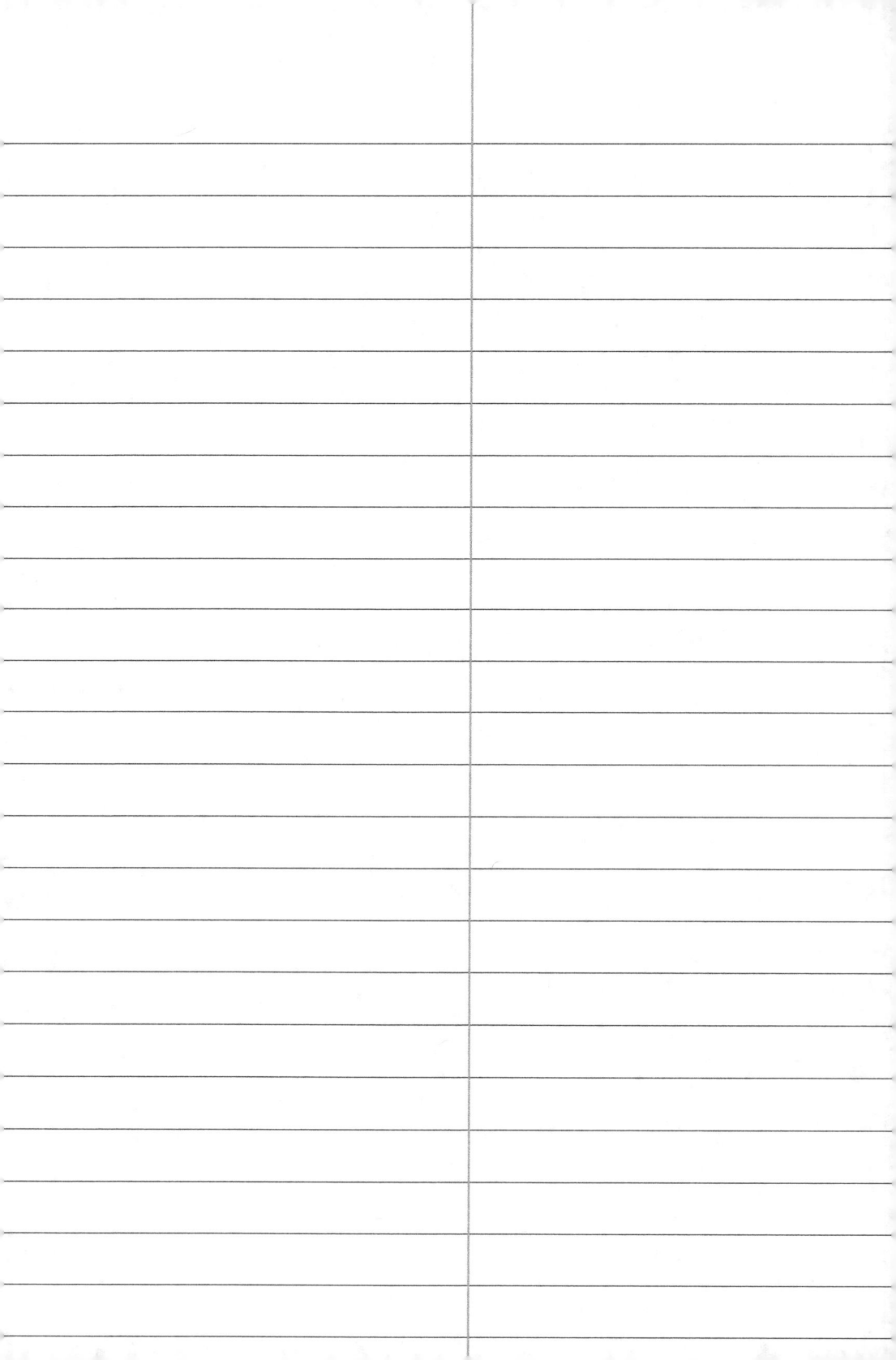

www.ingramcontent.com/pod-product-compliance
Lightning Source LLC
Chambersburg PA
CBHW071454220526
45472CB00003B/797